BUTCH CASSIDY

AND "THE WILD BUNCH"

ERIN DELFOE & E.W. ALLRED

D1707420

THE WAYSIDE BOOKSHOP

Published by Apricot Press
Box 1611
American Fork, Utah
84003

books@apricotpress.com
www.apricotpress.com

ISBN 1-885027-24-9

Cover Design & Layout by David Mecham
Printed in the United States of America

Preface

Few topics in American history generate as much interest as do outlaws and gunfighters of the old west. The names of many of these outlaws are legendary: Butch Cassidy and the Sundance Kid, Doc Holliday, Jesse James, Billy The Kid and Wyatt Earp to name a few. These men and others like them, epitomize the image of the Wild West. However, much of the popular legends surrounding them are not true or are greatly exaggerated. Unfortunately, because so much time has passed and the players have died, it is sometimes impossible to distinguish between truth and fiction. Here we attempt to describe the known facts about some of the famous outlaws, but more specifically an outlaw known as Butch Cassidy, as accurately as possible.

We hope you enjoy it.

An Environment for Lawlessness

First, let's create the setting. Let's look at what kind of environment created outlaws and gunfighters. There are a number of factors.

After Louis and Clark completed their amazing journey and exploration of the American West in 1806 and the results were published, white settlers began coming to exploit the land's enormous resources. At first there were only a few, missionaries and fur trappers mostly, but the trickle of emigration grew until ultimately, it became a flood.

The Indians

Ill equipped to deal with the Europeans' superior weapons and technology anyway, the Indian tribes were decimated by diseases for which they had no natural immunity. The vast majority died of small pox, measles, whooping cough, influenza or cholera. While the American Indians were a factor throughout most of the nineteenth century, they were culturally unequipped in the first place, and, thanks to this huge decline in population, in no

1

condition to give structure or social organization to such a vast area as the American West. So, for over half-a-century there was no government strong enough to guarantee law and safety for citizens in most areas. The first settlers who arrived just had to do whatever they could to protect their lives and property and dispense justice. Therefore, might made right.

In the eyes of European-Americans, this open land was free to anyone who could take it and hold on to it. Many of the settlers were law abiding men and women moving to the West hoping to find a better opportunity with wide open spaces and land for their families, or to exploit the other natural resources. However, many of the emigrants were refugees, dangerous men, economic failures, mentally ill, social misfits and criminals who were leaving the more populated East in order to escape troubles with the law. Some had come west to escape a failed marriage, which may have plagued them in more civilized Eastern society. Whatever a man's problems, out West it was a simple thing to change one's name and start over, or just disappear.

Because many law-abiding citizens were unskilled in gunplay, law enforcement, and soldiering, they were often desperate to find anyone who could provide for them a sense of security. Often times the lawman in one town was a fugitive of justice wanted in another.

The Civil War

The Civil War also contributed to the general lawlessness and brutality in the late 19th century. Displacement of thousands of former Southern Civil War soldiers, many of whom had experienced devastating emotional traumas, brought large numbers of men out West. Many had lost everything economically; some were wanted by the law for war crimes. Others couldn't accept the fact that the war was lost and they harbored bitter feelings against the government, which now controlled the South. Some were mentally ill, most likely suffering from what is now known as post-traumatic stress disorder. Still some had been unable to forgive soldiers who had fought for the other side in the great conflict. Many of the best-known Texas bad men began their careers killing what they called belligerent Negroes and their sympathizers.

As victory in that bitter conflict swung toward the Union forces, Confederate troops broke away rather than surrender. Some of these renegade bands continued fighting, harassing northern troops whenever they could, as well as attacking unprotected frontier settlements and killing those who held allegiance to the Union.

The Civil War ended but there was no turning back for some of the renegade soldiers. They survived because they had the support of many of the residents living on the frontier. Many of them were former Confederate soldiers who had returned home and found their farms and families ravaged by the war. The outlaw gangs rode against the tight-fisted banks, the rich stagecoach lines and monopolistic railroad companies. They became heroes to the legions of more peaceful men who admired the rebellious nature of the gunfighters, especially those who would fight against the large institutions who they felt were exploiting them.

The Six Shooter

Technology also contributed to the outlaw legend. In 1851, Samuel Colt introduced his 6-shooter revolver, the Colt 45. Thanks to brisk sales of the handgun, Remington and others quickly followed with various types and calibers of revolvers. Hundreds of thousands were sold during the Civil War because of their popularity with officers. Later on, these popular handguns made it simple to settle differences with bullets and helped contribute to the handgun culture that existed in the west.

Although the six shooter was easy to characterize as having been designed for the gunfight, as it is portrayed in movies and popular television shows, such face-to-face fair gun fights were rare, if they existed at all. As noted before, there was no code of chivalry in the American West. In reality, most men who were killers preferred the safe approach of sneaking up behind an unsuspecting victim and shooting him in the back or cutting his throat. When there were fights, which ended in someone being killed, they were usually murders or out-of-control brawls with no rules.

Although six-shooters were involved in many such brawls, instead of lying in the arms of his girl as the last of his life's blood oozed out, the majority of victims were doctored back to health and lived to fight another day.

Of course the vastness and wildness of the unsettled west also contributed to lawlessness. With deserts, badlands, mountains, forests, and poor communication, there were so many places for outlaws to hide that those

4

who enforced the laws faced daunting obstacles. Fugitives of justice one step ahead of the law could hide out in any number of places.

These factors and more combined to create a fascinating, dangerous, explosive and sometimes romantic era, which caused legends of outlaws like Butch Cassidy to grow in his own time and ours.

Around the turn of the 19th century the free-roaming gunfighters found the wild country could no longer hide them. Technology, in the form of telegraphs, telephones, trains, and automobiles cut off escape routes. Even though the era of the gunfighter had drawn to a close, writers and moviemakers, using the colorful backdrop of the Old West, turned frontier gunfighters into larger-than-life folk heroes, heroes who will never die.

Butch Cassidy

Robert Leroy Parker, A.K.A. Butch Cassidy, was one of those classic rogue, outlaw bandits of the Old West. He took advantage of nearly all of the tools available to him, and was a master of using the media to build support among the common people.

His life story began in Central Utah, in a small town called Beaver, where he was born to a Mormon family on April 13, 1866. Robert Parker, grandfather of Butch, was a Mormon emigrant, traveling with a handcart company in 1856. His particular company left late in the season and the snows of early October caught them at South Pass, near the end of the Wind River Range in western Wyoming. Parker was the leader of the group and a strong man. He broke the

Robert Leroy Parker, Butch Cassidy, 1893, Wyoming State
Penitentiary.

Used by permission, Utah State Historical Society.
All rights reserved. Photo no. 11917

6

trail, making it easier for the others to follow. With him came his wife and family of small children. One morning Parker was found dead, frozen to death in his bedroll. His wife and oldest son, Maximillian, then just 12, dug the grave and moved on, making it to the Salt Lake Valley. Maximillian continued faithfully in the church and helped other emigrants make their way from Missouri to Utah. The family moved to Beaver and there Maximillian met Ann Cambell. They were married and had a son named Robert Leroy Parker, who would later become the infamous Butch Cassidy. Soon after his birth, the family moved over the mountain ridge to the east, to a town called Circleville.

Maximillian Parker residence in Circleville, Utah.

7

Early Troubles

Robert's first run-in with the law came early, when he was about 13 years old. He rode into town to buy a pair of jeans. When he arrived he found the store was closed, so he let himself in, took the jeans and left a note pledging to return with the money. The storekeeper wasn't impressed and called the authorities. Robert was humiliated over the affair and thus got his first bitter taste for the law.

In Circleville, at about the age of 16, he went to work for a local cattleman named Mike Cassidy. Cassidy taught the very impressionable young Robert how to shoot, rope and rustle cattle. At the time, due to a shortage of law officers and an abundance of wide-open spaces, it was relatively easy for a rancher to add to his herd by rustling cattle from other ranchers. Apparently, Mike Cassidy was in the habit of building up his herd in this way. Young Robert received on-the-job training in the field of cattle theft, and he eventually became Cassidy's right hand man. Robert, in his later years, took on the name Cassidy, probably to save embarrassment for his family and because of these early influences.

Soon Cassidy and Robert Parker left the ranch. They had run into difficulty with their neighbors and the law by siding with ranchers in a range war. Mike Cassidy had subsequently shot a Wyoming rancher and disappeared into hiding. While he was gone, young Roy Parker took over his ranching and rustling operations. It was at this time that he assumed the last name of "Cassidy." Mike Cassidy had also been a part of a gang of outlaws and because Robert was such a natural born leader he took over the gang in

8

Gunfight pass in Kane County, Wyoming, is similar to Hole
-in-the-Wall, a deep V-shaped canyon that provided refuge
to outlaws in 1880-90's. The inhabitants of the six cabins in
the valley were known as the "Hole In The Wall Gang."

Mike's absence. The gang headquartered out of Robbers Roost, a natural fortress located in one of the most desolate and isolated places on the planet the southwest corner of Utah. Robert had a certain knack for locating such areas, as he would later do in Wyoming at the Hole-In-The-Wall. He and his fellow outlaws could hide out or hold off the law in these natural strongholds.

Learning the Ropes

Robert Cassidy continued a busy schedule of "developing" his herd through every means at his disposal. He also experimented with bigger, quicker money by robbing a few banks in isolated communities and in early 1887, at the age of 21, met Bill and Tom McCarty and decided to join their gang and rob a train.

On November 3, 1887 the new gang stopped the Denver & Rio Grande express near Grand Junction, Colorado and when the guard refused to open the safe, Bill McCarty put a gun to his head and asked if he should kill the guard. The gang took a vote and voted not to end his life and the train went on its way.

After this failed attempt, Butch tried to make an honest living working as a cowboy and miner in Colorado and Utah, something he would try to do many times during his life of crime, but was never really successful. He changed his name to George, settled in Rock Springs, Wyoming and began working there as a butcher. This is where he acquired his nickname, "Butch."

In March 1889, the First National Bank of Denver was robbed of twenty one thousand dollars, and although no one was caught and charged with the robbery, Butch and his gang are credited with it. The story begins when a well-dressed businessman walked into the office of bank president David Moffat, declaring that the bank was about to be robbed.

The stranger took from his pocket a bottle containing clear liquid and announced to Moffat that the bottle contained nitroglycerin and he would blow the bank apart if Moffat did not follow his instructions. The stranger asked the trembling Moffat to write out a check for $21,000, then call in his cashier and ask him to cash it. Moffat did as he

McCormick and Co. Bank, similar to one of the banks robbed by Butch and Sundance.

11

was instructed. The cashier, although he suspected something was wrong, did as he was told.

After placing the money in a bag, the cashier handed it to the stranger who then disappeared out the front door of the bank.

Butch and his gang committed many robberies, but in the beginning, they had a lot to learn. In one instance Matt Warner, Tom McCarty and Butch had just robbed a bank and divided up the paper money. After divvying it up the outlaws rode through rain and snow to Star Valley, when they arrived at their cabin and took the now dried stacks of money from their saddlebags they got the shock of their lives. The bills could not be separated. Matt tried to peel a

Matt Warner (left) and Jim Peterson (right), "outlaws." Photo taken when Warner was hiding from Utah and Wyoming law officers in Meeker, Colorado.

few of the dry bills off the bundle but destroyed others in the process. Tom suggested that they soak the bundles in water through the night.

The next morning the three outlaws sat around the kitchen table and began separating the soggy bills. As they worked a bill loose they would attach it to the cabin wall to dry. It took them the better part of two days to get their bills separated, losing some in the process.

A few old-timers lucky enough to be invited inside their cabin reported that two walls were covered with bills and as the wrinkled bills dried out they would fall to the cabin floor. Matt and Tom gathered up the bills, which were now wrinkled and thicker than ordinary bills. Wrinkled bills that began circulating around Star Valley were known as "Tellurides" named after the town they were stolen from.

The boys were fast learners. On future bank jobs the outlaws kept their bills high and dry. If rivers were to be crossed on horseback, the saddle bags with the paper money were held high overhead.

Unfortunately, after this particular robbery the law was after them. The outlaws packed up their money and headed for the Colorado River.

The posse was right on their tails as they arrived at the Hite ferry, but there was a problem. The ferry was all the way on the other side of the river and the posse was closing in on the outlaws. Matt called out to the ferryman to bring the ferry across as fast as he could.

The ferrymen yelled back that it would take about five minutes, but the outlaws knew they couldn't wait that long, and decided that the ferryman needed a little incentive. Matt called out, "I'll bet you twenty dollars that you can't be here in two minutes." It was at that point that Butch pretended to pull out a pocket watch and yelled, "I'll give you twenty bucks if you can be here within two minutes, starting now.

The ferryman dug in his oars working twice as fast with each stroke. Twenty dollars was more than he would earn in a week at the ferry.

The posse appeared in the distance just as the ferry was arriving at the bank where the outlaws were waiting. Butch and his friends jumped onto the ferry and helped the sweat drenched ferryman row to the other side. Once on the other side, Butch paid the man his twenty dollars and the outlaws rode to freedom.

As noted above, one of the ways the outlaws escaped from the law was by hiding fresh horses along their escape route so they could outride the posse. Butch and his gang were always looking for the fastest horses around, so one day while taking a train ride, abut five miles outside of San Bernardino, California, Butch spotted some bleachers and a circular racetrack with a long straightaway. He found the conductor and asked him to let them off at the next town.

As they got off the train, McCarty asked why he had picked such a miserable little place to stop. Butch replied that he had seen what he was looking for. "And what's that?" asked McCartly. "A racetrack," replied Butch.

14

McCary didn't' understand until Butch explained; "What runs on a racetrack? Fast horses. Get it?" McCarty grinned. "I believe I'm getting the picture now." Butch and his gang bought as many fast race horses as they could afford.

Trying to Go Straight

We do have to give Butch some credit for attempting to go straight a number of times in his career. However, going straight was beyond his ability, because in 1893, Cassidy was arrested in Rock Springs, Wyoming for stealing a horse. Butch then met a man named Al Hainer and began an extortion racket in Colorado. They would sell local ranchers protection from rustlers but what the ranchers soon found out was that if they didn't pay the fee, it was Butch and Hainer who would rustle their cattle. Ranchers turned to John Chapman and Bob Calverly to track down the pair. When they caught up to the outlaws, Hainer was captured outside their cabin and tied to a tree. When Calverly entered the cabin where Butch was relaxing, guns began blazing and Cassidy was grazed with a bullet and knocked unconscious. He was then handcuffed and taken to the Lander County jail by Jim Miller, deputy sheriff and jailer. Butch would start his journey to the Territorial Prison in Laramie, Wyoming the next morning.

Deputy Miller had known Butch during his earlier days at Brown's Park. He had ridden with Butch and the others on several cattle rustling jobs, but when Miller met Elsie, the beautiful young woman who would become his wife, his outlaw days became just memories.

15

When Jim had asked for Elsie's hand in marriage, he had been told in no uncertain terms by Elsie that it was either, "Get an honest job or get lost."

When Butch arrived at Lander County jail he asked Miller if he could take his handcuffs off and let him have the night off to dispose of his belongings. He promised Jim he'd be back in the morning before they left for Laramie.

Miller replied, "Are you crazy? You and I are good friends but you are a prisoner of the state of Wyoming. Do you think I'm clear crazy?"

"No," Butch replied, "I've never thought you were clear crazy. Undo these cuffs and tell me what time we're heading for the big house."

Miller replied that it was about six in the morning, so Butch asked him again to let him go for the night promising to be back by morning. Miller and Butch had always trusted each other during their rustling days but this was different. Miller wondered what would happen if Butch didn't show up. Butch responded by saying, "Have I ever let you down in the past?"

Miller unlocked the handcuffs and said, "Damn your hide. You'd better be back before first light or we'll get a posse and shoot you on sight."

Butch thanked him and told him that because of his generosity he would help him with his problem of trying to fit five convicts and two deputies into the coach to take to prison.

Six a.m. arrived the next morning and when Miller arrived at the jail, Butch was there with his feet up on Miller's desk with a big smile on his face.

Butch and four other convicts would start their journey toward Laramie. They would be guarded by Miller and two other Deputies. When the coach arrived, Butch explained that they had two problems. First of all, the prisoners couldn't be cuffed with their hands behind their backs because of the long ride. The deputies immediately uncuffed the prisoner's hands and re-cuffed them in front. Second, Butch explained that with their hands in front, five mean outlaws could easily overpower one deputy, which would be all that was in the coach because the other one had to ride up front.

Butch said that if he were in charge he would take his handcuffs off so that he could ride in front and so the other deputy could fit in with the prisoners.

"Damn your hide," Said Miller. If anything goes wrong, I'm holding you responsible."

Arriving at the prison, Warden Adams noticed only four prisoners in shackles. When he asked about the fifth man, the sheriff pointed out that Butch was the other prisoner but was not shackled. Warden Adams wanted to know the reason. Butch leaned over to Adams and whispered loud enough for all to hear. "I guess its honor among thieves." Warden Adams was not amused. Miller said that if Butch gave his word that he would not escape, you could count on it. Butch had a reputation of being a man of his word.

Creating the Wild Bunch

After a year and a half in the prison, Butch's sentence was complete. He applied for and got a hearing with Governor William Richards. As the story goes, he told the governor a tale about how he intended to go to Colorado to tend some land he had there. The Governor asked Cassidy to promise that if he were pardoned, he would quit rustling cattle, but Cassidy said: "Can't do that governor, because if I gave you my word, I'd only have to break it." He did promise the governor that if he were given a pardon, he would not commit any crimes in Wyoming. Unbelievably, the governor signed the order and on January 19, 1896, Butch Cassidy walked out of prison a free man, but not before meeting one of the central figures of his future gang: Harry Longbaugh, better known as The Sundance Kid.

Upon his release, Butch promptly rode to the Hole-In-The-Wall where he formed his gang that would become famously known as "The Wild Bunch." Although today we know the outlaw band as The Wild Bunch, during it's heyday, the band was known in the newspapers as the Hole-in-the-Wall gang, the Train Robber's Syndicate, Butch Cassidy's gang, Kid Curry's gang, the Powder Springs gang, and the Robber's Roost gang. The first recorded use of the "Wild Bunch" in reference to Butch, Sundance and their pals was in a 1902 Pinkerton memorandum to the American Bankers Association. The headline-friendly name was soon picked up by the newspapers, undoubtedly with help from the detective agency. Ironically, by then the gang was no more. The term was used generically in the Old West to mean a group of cowboys on a spree or a herd of free-roaming horses.

18

Although the gang was known as the Wild Bunch, Butch, Sundance, and their comrades in arms were never much of a bunch. Although perhaps as many as thirty outlaws participated in crimes attributed to the gang, hardly any of them committed more than a couple of holdups with each other. Furthermore, how many crimes they actually participated in is unclear, inasmuch as famous outlaws are often blamed for others deeds.

Even though the group wasn't much of a gang, there are some members that were associated with the name, "The Wild Bunch". They are as follows: Harry "Sundance Kid" Longbaugh; (nicknamed possibly from Sundance, Wyoming where he was caught as a horse thief), Ben "The

Patrick Coughlin (left) and Fred George (right), members of "The Wild Bunch."

Laura Bullion, female member of "The Wild Bunch."

Tall Texan" Kilpatrick; known as the lady killer of the group, Bill Carver; the quick draw, Camila "Deaf Charlie" Hanks; partly deaf in one ear, Elza Lay (a.k.a. William McGinnis); one time geology student, Tom "Peep" ODay; court jester, Joe Chancellor; skilled safecracker and poker player, Jim Lowe; bartender, Jesse Lindley; the dapper dresser, William "Bill" Cruzan; best horse thief, Dave Atkins; already on the run when he joined the group, Walter, Wat the Watcher, Punteney; Jack of all trades, Willard E. Christiansen (a.k.a Matt Warner); part of McCarty's gang, Bob Meeks; cowboy, Laura Bullion; rode for a while, Etta Place; prostitute, Annie Rogers; a favorite of Kid Curry, Lillie Davis; a prostitute, and Harvey "Kid Curry" Logan. Regardless of their public persona, they were, in reality, a group of hardened, savvy, vicious criminals.

Changing with the Times

At the time of the formation of Hole-In-The-Wall Gang, the railroad, telegraph, and other new technologies were shrinking the wild frontier of Butch's youth. However, an increasing population, while reducing the wide-open spaces, also created additional opportunities for a thief. Thanks to their years of experience, The Wild Bunch pioneered some technological innovations of their own in the field of robbery and crime. For example, in order to outrun possies, they carefully planned their robberies and placed horses at intervals so they could ride fresh mounts and keep moving far beyond where law enforcement would ever expect them to get to. By the time the law could catch up or figure it out, the trail would again be cold.

Like many icons in Western society, the concept of the gunslinger was in large part created by the media. The telegraph, the train, and later the telephone made transmission of their stories quick and easy. Often, the entire country read in fascination the stories of the exploits of one desperado or another. Because of the public's fascination with violence and crime, the newspapers and other writers met the demand by rushing news of the latest crime or robbery to an anxiously waiting public faster than had been possible at any earlier time in history, sometimes filling in the gaps of factual information with speculation, and often embellishing the facts with wild tales to make stories read better.

A brash boldness and a touch of class, combined with the spread of communications technology and newspapers soon made it possible for Butch to create his Robin Hood-type hero's image. Led by Butch, the gang played the newspapers like violins in order to garner public support and make their hiding and escapes easier. The gentleman bandit aura was fostered by The Wild Bunch, which even posed for group photographs creating considerable support from common people. This support was essential to their escape at critical times.

Surprisingly, many outlaws had the support of the public. There was an aura of romance built up around them and Americans have always had an affinity for brazen and courageous rogues who they perceived to be underdogs. Many Americans aided and hid the outlaws because they identified with them, were cheering for them, and they wanted to help them beat the system. Many common people detested the institutions they were robbing. It was

The Wild Bunch photo, 1900. Left to Right: Standing, Bill Carver and Harvey Logan ("Kid Curry") Seated, Harry Longbough ("Sundance Kid"), Ben Kilpatrick ("Tall Texan"), and Robert Leroy Parker ("Butch Cassidy").

usually tough for lawmen to get any help from locals who had a sense of "us against them". Some outlaws like The Wild Bunch understood this phenomenon and exploited it to the fullest using a sympathetic public to help them escape over and over again. They used the pictures they had taken and placed them in newspapers to build their legend and increase popular support.

This was particularly true where there were large numbers of Southern sympathizers, since Southerners considered the Northern Bankers who bankrolled the Union during the Civil War, the enemy. They would do whatever they could to get back at them. Civil War survivors from the Confederacy were also anxious to believe that poor southern or Western boys were being persecuted in some way, thereby justifying their crusade against the establishment. Often an outlaw's popularity depended upon which region of the country he hailed from.

Part of the romance gunslingers built up over the years centered on the notion of the Good Guy who wears the white hat, who is filled with righteous indignation and chivalry. He risks his life and uses his gun-fighting talents to defend the weak and helpless. Old time novelists created this image, examples of which include the Lone Ranger, or Marshall Dillon. These were portrayed as defenders of women and children. These legends come mostly from writers' imaginations. Historic fact does not back up this fantasy. The truth places real outlaws and gunfighters somewhere between a ruthless, callous killer indifferent to human suffering and life, and a desperate person doing whatever he must do to stay alive in a wild and tough land. As in other times of anarchy, the weak and helpless were taken advantage of by the strong and the ruthless; this included gunslingers and rogue bandits like The Wild Bunch.

Even though most members of The Hole In The Wall gang were in fact cold-blooded killers, tales of always shooting at the horses of their pursuers and not riders circulated throughout the West. Butch himself bragged that he had never killed a man. When stories of blowing up rail cars with dynamite and leaving the faithful guard inside shaken but unharmed as thousands of dollars floated through the air were published, the legend grew.

A Closer Look at Butch

Butch was also known for his generosity, laughter, and love of practical jokes. After entering a Wyoming saloon, he noticed a local drunk asleep in a chair tipped up against the wall. Butch first shot out the rungs of the chair one by one, and then shot the tips of the legs until it collapsed while still holding its slumbering occupant. Legend has it that at this time, Butch's custom was to award the objects of his practical jokes a twenty-dollar gold piece. Unfortunately history doesn't recollect whether the drunk woke up in time to collect his prize.

Many stories of Butch's generosity circulated. For example: One day as Butch and two friends were riding into Salina, Utah they noticed a farmer starting to move large rocks in what appeared to be the foundation for a home. The ever-friendly Butch rode over to the farmer who was covered with dust and sweat from lifting the rocks, and began a conversation. He said that they were looking for a place to stay for the night and wondered if they could make a deal with the farmer for room and board. Butch offered to help the farmer with his foundation for the day and the farmer agreed. Butch's two friends, one of which happened to be the infamous Sundance Kid, weren't very excited, but decided to help anyway.

The three outlaws worked until dark digging trenches and putting large rocks in place. When they finished they

25

went up to the house and bedded down for the night. The next day, Butch surprised his two friends, and the farmer by offering to spend an extra day helping with the foundation.

Another story of Butch's generosity goes as follows; After an extremely severe winter, thousands of head of livestock froze to death or starved because of the deep fall of snow. To make matters worse, almost everyone was stricken with the epidemic now known as flu, leaving no one to look after the animals or care for the sick.

According to the story, during this epidemic, Butch obtained home remedies from a woman who lived on a ranch four miles away from his, and ministered to his sick neighbors.

The late 1800's were a time of romance, and Butch and his gang definitely capitalized on this. In music this period is known as the romantic era. As the frontier became thoroughly mapped and explored and as civilization began to tame this former wilderness, a sense of nostalgia came into vogue. Painters and writers romanticized The Old West. Many writers borrowed myths and facts from earlier times and incorporated them into this era. For example, for hundreds of years European men fought duels in order to defend their honor. These duels were fought according to strict rules and each participant brought a "Second" along to make sure it was a fair fight. Since the fight was to defend honor, men of honor would never consider stooping to cheat in any way. This idea of chivalry was borrowed by writers of films and novels during this romantic era and pinned on some outlaws and gunfighters to glamorize them. Unfortunately, old West gunfights were nothing like this;

however, Butch, more than any outlaw up until this time, used these romantic images to his advantage.

Butch's image as a Robin Hood figure was furthered by the story of a 16-year-old boy named Harry Ogden from Escalante, Utah. The story states that Ogden had spent his entire savings on a horse and a sixty-dollar saddle. One day while out riding along the border of Robber's Roost in 1898, an outlaw forced him off his horse, gave the boy a swift kick in the pants, then rode off with it. About three weeks later, Ogden received a visit at his home in Escalante from Butch Cassidy and the outlaw who had stolen his horse. When Cassidy asked Ogden if he had lost a horse, the boy identified the man and his horse. Butch then ordered the outlaw off the horse and told him to start walking toward a distant gap in the hills and keep on going. He then said, "We don't have any room in this country for a man who will mistreat a young boy."

Aside from stories like this one it didn't help the law that most people who knew him described Cassidy as an agreeable fellow with a sense of humor, generous with his associates, and quick to make friends with children. He was described by many as a good man who engaged in a little too much gambling, but seldom drank to excess. An old timer once summed it up this way: "I wouldn't want to have been in the teller's cage when he came through the door of a bank, but if I ever met him in a saloon, I sure would have bought him a drink."

Despite his popularity, the fact was that Butch was an outlaw running from the law. The harsh desert of Southwestern Wyoming and Eastern Utah is a rugged and desolate place. Only desperate men with grit and a thorough knowledge of the area could expect to survive for long there. Butch was such a man and he knew the area well. He and his band located one of the most forbidding landscapes in the world as their hideout when the heat was on. The newspapers named it "Robbers' Roost" further adding to the mystique of the Wild Bunch. Here a handful of outlaws could hold off a virtual army of law enforcement personnel indefinitely, if they were lucky enough to find them.

The gang was responsible for a number of high-profile robberies, but in an attempt to live up to the promise he had made to Governor William Richards, the gang robbed the Montpelier, Idaho Bank on August 13, 1896 instead of robbing banks in Wyoming. This was a successful robbery because Butch had scouted out the town and the bank for weeks in advance. They netted about $7,165. There next hit was a mining camp at Castle Gate, in Carbon County Utah and since they had made so much money between the two, the allure of going straight once again became strong.

Butch rode to New Mexico and got a job as a cowboy. It was not long, though, when his money ran out and he was back at Hole-In-The-Wall planning his next job with the Wild Bunch.

On June 2, 1899, the gang stopped the Union Pacific's Overland Flyer. In a remote area, the gang used a pile of wood on the tracks to force the train to stop. They boarded the train and shook down the passengers for cash, watches, and jewelry. They then ordered the engineer to uncouple the express car and move the rest of the train across a small trestle. When the engineer refused, he was pistol-whipped and the trestle was then blown up, leaving the vulnerable express car by itself. Inside the car was a guard named Woodcock. When he was ordered to open the door, the prompt answer was, "Come in and get me!" The gang then placed another charge against the rail car door. The car was blown to pieces and it sent a badly injured Woodcock flying to the ground. When one of the members of the gang was preparing to send the guard, "to hell," Cassidy interfered, telling the others that a man with that much nerve deserved to live. They spared Woodcock's life and began packing up the scattered $30,000 in bank notes.

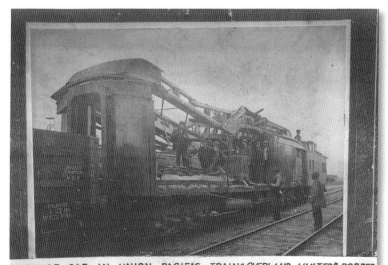

BAGGAGE CAR IN UNION PACIFIC TRAIN "OVERLAND LIMITED" ROBBED AT WILCOX, WYOMING, JUNE 1 1899 - - - WILLIAM STOREY, CONDUCTOR.

Remains of a railway car after the Wilcox robbery.

29

The Beginning of the End

Nothing lasts forever. The Wild Bunch's popularity and notoriety was a two-edged sword. The railroads who were embarrassed because of the publicity about their inability to protect shipments of money and bullion, determined to spare no expense to bring the group to justice. They hired the famous Pinkerton Detective Agency to track the Wild Bunch down and bring them to justice. After a few close scrapes, a savvy Butch Cassidy determined that it was best to split up the gang and take their chances individually. Butch and his now best buddy, Harry Longbaugh, known as the Sundance Kid headed back to the Hole.

After the split Butch worked hard to foster a clean, good-guy image and even though in an interview with a newspaper, Butch insisted that he had never killed a man, the fact was that the gang was full of vicious, desperate killers. Harry Tracy, who without Butch's PR skills turned out to be a bad engineer of his own personal public relations, claimed, "I kill only those who get in my way."

It was said of Harvey Logan, otherwise known as "Kid Curry", "He would ride 1000 miles to kill a man." The truth is, Butch was never convicted or charged with killing anyone. Whether he did or didn't personally pull the trigger, there were numerous people murdered by the gang during the crime sprees they carried out. This made him guilty of murder in the eyes of the law.

Most of the members of the gang were hunted down and either killed or placed in prison, but the remaining members again decided to rob the Union Pacific Train at Tipton,

30

Pinkerton's National Detective Agency.

FOUNDED BY ALLAN PINKERTON, 1850.

OFFICES.

ROBT. A. PINKERTON, New York. } Principals
WM. A. PINKERTON, Chicago. }

GEO. D. BANGS, General Manager, New York
ALLAN PINKERTON, Assistant General Manager.

JOHN CORNISH, Gen'l Sup't., Eastern Division, New York.
EDWARD S. GAYLOR, Gen'l Sup't., Middle Division, Chicago.
JAMES McPARLAND, Gen'l Supt., Western Division, Denver.

Attorneys—GUTHRIE, CRAVATH & HENDERSON, New York.

TELEPHONE CONNECTION.

REPRESENTING THE AMERICAN BANKERS' ASSOCIATION.

$4,000.00 REWARD.

CIRCULAR No. 2.

DENVER, Colo., January 24th, 1902.

THE FIRST NATIONAL BANK OF WINNEMUCCA, Nevada, a member of THE AMERICAN BANKERS' ASSOCIATION, was robbed of $32,640 at the noon hour, September 19th, 1900, by three men who entered the bank and "held up" the cashier and four other persons. Two of the robbers carried revolvers and a third a Winchester rifle. They compelled the five persons to go into the inner office of the bank while the robbery was committed.

At least $31,000 was in $20 gold coin; $1,200 in $5 and $10 gold coin; the balance in currency, including one $50 bill.

Since the issuance of our first circular, dated Denver, Colo., May 15th, 1901, it has been positively determined that two of the men who committed this robbery were:

1. GEORGE PARKER, alias "BUTCH" CASSIDY, alias GEORGE CASSIDY, alias INGERFIELD.
2. HARRY LONGBAUGH, alias "KID" LONGBAUGH, alias HARRY ALONZO, alias "THE SUNDANCE KID."

PARKER and LONGBAUGH are members of the HARVEY LOGAN alias "KID" CURRY band of bank and train (express) "hold up" robbers.

For the arrest, detention and surrender to an authorized officer of the State of Nevada of each or any one of the men who robbed the FIRST NATIONAL BANK OF WINNEMUCCA, the following rewards are offered:

BY THE FIRST NATIONAL BANK OF WINNEMUCCA: $1,000 for each robber.
Also 25 per cent., in proportionate shares, on all money recovered.

BY THE AMERICAN BANKERS' ASSOCIATION: $1,000 for each robber.
This reward to be paid on proper identification of either PARKER or LONGBAUGH.

Persons furnishing information leading to the arrest of either or all of the robbers will be entitled to share in the reward.

The outlaws, whose photographs, descriptions and histories appear on this circular MAY ATTEMPT TO CIRCULATE or be in possession of the following described NEW INCOMPLETE BANK NOTES of the NATIONAL BANK OF MONTANA and THE AMERICAN NATIONAL BANK, both of HELENA, MONT., which were stolen by members of the HARVEY LOGAN, alias "KID" CURRY BAND, from the GREAT NORTHERN (RAILWAY) EXPRESS No. 3, near Wagner, Mont., July 3rd, 1901, by "hold up" methods.

$40,000. INCOMPLETE NEW BANK NOTES of the NATIONAL BANK OF MONTANA (Helena, Montana), $24,000 of which was in ten dollar bills and $16,000 of which was in twenty dollar bills.

Serial Number 1201 to 2000 inclusive;
Government Number-Y 934349 to 935148 inclusive;
Charter Number 5671.

$500. INCOMPLETE BANK NOTES of AMERICAN NATIONAL BANK (Helena, Montana), $300 of which was in ten dollar bills and $200 of which was in twenty dollar bills.

Serial Number 3423 to 3432 inclusive;
Government Number V-662781 to V-662770 inclusive;
Charter Number 4396.

THESE INCOMPLETE BANK NOTES LACKED THE SIGNATURES OF THE PRESIDENTS AND CASHIERS OF THE BANKS NAMED, AND MAY BE CIRCULATED WITHOUT SIGNATURES OR WITH FORGED SIGNATURES.

Chiefs of Police, Sheriffs, Marshals and Constables receiving copy of this circular should furnish a copy of the above described stolen currency to banks, bankers, money brokers, gambling houses, pool room keepers and keepers of disorderly houses, and request their co-operation in the arrest of any person or persons presenting any of these bills.

THE UNITED STATES TREASURY DEPARTMENT REFUSES TO REDEEM THESE STOLEN UNSIGNED OR IMPROPERLY SIGNED NOTES.

Officers are warned to have sufficient assistance and be fully armed, when attempting to arrest either of these outlaws, as they are always heavily armed, and will make a determined resistance before submitting to arrest, not hesitating to kill, if necessary.

Foreign ministers and consuls receiving copy of this circular are respectfully
Postmasters receiving this circular are requested to place same in hands of reliable

Charles Angelo Siringo joined The Pinkerton National Detective Agency in 1855 and spent four years in pursuit of Butch Cassidy throughout Colorado, Utah, and New

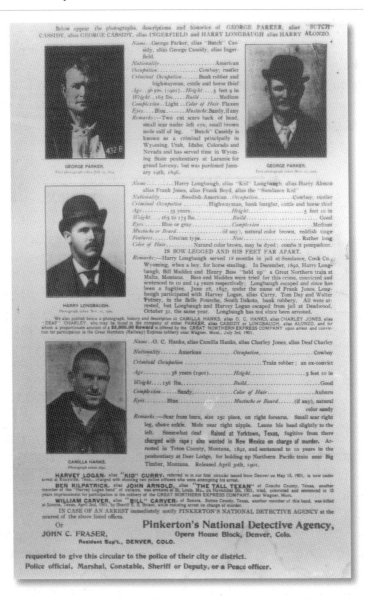

Mexico - even pretending to be an outlaw to infiltrate Robber's Roost, Utah. He never did catch Butch.

Wyoming on August 29, 1900. Once again, they ordered the guard to open the door to the express car and much to their amazement, it was Woodcock and he again refused to open the door. Butch instructed the engineer to tell that, "iron-headed Woodcock that if he doesn't open the door, we'll blow him and the car sky-high!"

After the engineer pleaded with Woodcock, he relented and opened the door. The take on this robbery was $50,000, the largest haul they had ever made. Butch and Sundance and the remainder of the Wild Bunch were once again on the run. Again the Union Pacific hired the most aggressive lawman they could find, Joe Lefors, to track them down. After many months of running and chasing, the lawman lost them at their favorite hideout, the Hole-In-The-Wall. There were several other robberies in the couple years that followed, but finally the heat got to be too much for Butch and Sundance.

Life on the Lamb

The two outlaws and close friends rode to Ft. Worth, Texas to relax in Fannie Porter's brothel. It is here that Sundance ran into Etta (Ethel) Place, an attractive brunette who longed for adventure. The three of them left for New York to have some fun, stay in the nicest hotels and enjoy the good life for a while. In late 1901, they moved on to Buenos Aires and settled in southern Argentina where they took the names James Ryan and Mr. and Mrs. Harry Place. They built a cabin in the Cholila Valley and began ranching. Butch once again showed his creativity and resourcefulness in building his cabin. He decided that he didn't want to pay for his logs so he cooked up a plan. Butch found a Mill that

ETTA PLACE.
Mrs. Kid Longbough.
of
" Wild Bunch."

Etta Place, January, 1901. Shortly thereafter, she left for Argentina with the Sundance Kid.

Erin Delfoe E.W. Allred

was close to a river and waited for the next big storm. When it hit, Butch ran to the mill. The water was pouring out of the sky and lightening and thunder was flashing all around. He knew that the owners of the mill would be inside drinking and playing cards because no one would be out in that kind of weather.

Butch worked his way down to the stack of logs he'd chosen earlier, glad to see they hadn't been touched. Carefully he shifted a few logs from near the bottom of the pile without disturbing the rest. Then he unwrapped his oil-skin and canvas package and worked to place the dynamite, blasting cap and fuse inside the hole he had created in the logs.

Later, as he was riding away on his horse, he heard the dynamite and watched as logs flew everywhere. The noise was a little louder than the thunder but the storm was so fierce Butch figured that the owners wouldn't suspect a thing.

Early that afternoon the first log was spotted coming down the river. Butch worked all afternoon getting the logs onto the riverbank. He figured that if the logs were at least sixteen feet long he would need around thirty logs for an eight by sixteen foot cabin. By sundown there were no more logs in the river. Butch counted thirty-four logs. Butch would now have a place of his own.

A few weeks later he ran into the owner of the mill and was surprised when he said, "We had the craziest storm I've ever seen in my eighteen years since coming west. Lightning hit one pile of logs, blowing some clear across

35

the river. First lightening I've ever seen that left a hole in the ground."

For three years they lived a peaceful life, but this life would not last forever. Although Sundance may have been married, Butch probably never was, at least no records to that affect have ever been found, but he welcomed the company of women and seldom was without their companionship, even when in hiding.

The Outlaw's Fate

But what ever happened to the Wild Bunch? After Butch and Sundance went to South America the Wild Bunch quickly disintegrated. Without their leader they were helpless. There was no one left with the ability to plan, organize, and execute increasingly more complicated robberies. They never again gathered for a raid, and their previously spectacular exploits soon became history, kept alive by hundreds of legendary tales repeated wherever cowboys gathered. Most of the Bunch left to try and become respectable ranchers and soon the Robber's Roost was deserted.

One of the most fascinating aspects to the legend of Butch Cassidy is whatever became of him. In the 1968 Robert Redford, Paul Neuman movie, Cassidy and Sundance are shown in Bolivia facing down an entire army and going out in a blaze of glory. But almost everything you read on the subject shows their death in a different way.

Many believe that Butch and Sundance returned to their old outlaw ways in Argentina. They started to hold up banks, trains, and mine payrolls. They became as infamous in South America as they had been earlier in the United States. It was about that time that Etta returned to the United States and faded into oblivion. On December 19, 1905 Butch and Sundance robbed the bank at Villa Mercedes, Argentina. They were pursued into Chile with several possies chasing them. The two then split up for some time with Butch going to work at the Concordia Tin Mines in Bolivia. The Sundance Kid joined Butch at the Mines later and they soon quit and held up the Aramayo, Francke & Cia payroll near Tupiza, Bolivia. They escaped into the mountains with about 15,000 Bolivians and the mining company pack mule.

The Pinkertons tried to gather funds to send a posse after Butch and Sundance in Argentina, but the American banks and railroads declined to chip in. The agency had to be satisfied with arranging for WANTED posters in Spanish and warning the Buenos Aires police chief: "It is our firm belief that it is only a question of time until these men commit some desperate robbery in the Argentine Republic. They are all thorough plainsmen and horsemen, riding from 600 to 1,000 miles after committing a robbery. If there are reported to you any bank or train hold up robberies or any other similar crimes, you will find that they were undoubtedly committed by these men."

Butch and Sundance then went to the town of San Vincente and found a place to stay. Someone there notified the soldiers that two American strangers had arrived and the soldiers prepared a trap. A huge gun battle ensued between

Butch, Sundance and the military, which lasted all night long. The next morning, after the shooting had died down for some time, the soldiers entered the house where the outlaws had been holed up and found Butch and Sundance sitting inside, both with bullet wounds to the head. It is speculated that when it was obvious that they would not escape, one man killed the other and then turned the gun on himself. They were buried later that day, but dug up two weeks later to be positively identified by Carlos Pero.

You may think the story ends here, but the predominance of evidence and the majority of scholars now believe that their death in South America was staged. In fact, the men who identified the two bodies had never seen Butch and Sundance and it is believed that another pair of outlaws were killed by the troops and that Cassidy and Sundance purposefully let it be known they had been killed. Butch, after living his miserable life on the run for so many years, most likely found a way to successfully disappear for a decade or so until the heat died down.

He is said to have then somehow returned from South America to Southern California or some even say the Pacific North West where he tried a number of legitimate businesses, including furniture and appliance business, which failed. He had sporadic contacts with members of his family during this time and even tried to interest a number of publishers in his memoirs. This, too, failed.

Among those making the claim that they saw Cassidy was his sister Lula Parker Betenson who claimed that he came for a visit in the fall of 1925. He supposedly told members of his family that a friend, Percy Seibert, from the

Concordia Tin Mines near San Vicente, Bolivia, identified the two bodies as being those of him and Sundance. Cassidy figured that Seibert did this so he could make a new start for himself without being chased by the law, either in the United States or in South America. Apparently he had expressed such a desire to Seibert on several occasions.

In addition to his family's claims, many friends of his insisted that he had returned for a visit in the 1930's. Emma Allene Savage Riddle recalled her experience in her autobiography, "One day I went with Dad to visit Elijah Moore. There were several other men at his home when we arrived. Elijah introduced us to them and one of then was an outlaw by the name of Leroy Parker, alias Butch Cassidy. This was after Butch had been reported killed in Bolivia, South America. I was in awe of the man, thinking I had met a real honest-to-goodness outlaw."

Another widely accepted ending to the Butch Cassidy story is that he escaped and started using an assumed identity, William Thadeus Phillips. Butch passed himself off as a mechanical engineer from Des Moines, Iowa. The following spring he married Gertrude Livesay and the couple moved to Globe, Arizona. There he worked as a mercenary in the Mexican Revolution. From Arizona, the Phillips went to Spokane, Washington, and started an office equipment company. In the early 1930's Phillips sold the business because of the great depression. In this version, cancer claimed Butch's life instead of a gun.

"The Butch Cassidy Lives" story is so resilient it rivals Elvis sightings; so here are a few more endings. Choose for yourself if you believe they have any merit.

There is a wild story that Hiram BeBee, doing life in Utah State Prison for killing a city marshal in 1945, was, in fact, The Sundance Kid. If physical features were any indication, BeBee would have had to shrink substantially. Sundance was from 5-foot-10 to 6 feet tall; Hiram BeBee at the time of his arrest was 5-foot-5.

Author Larry Pointers contends that Cassidy lived out his days in America as William T. Phillips, a Spokane businessman, and died in 1937.

Idaho mechanic Budd Anderton claimed that Butch spent his last four or five years in relative seclusion in Richfield, Utah, where he died and was buried in the 1930's.

There is also an account given in the fall of 1991 by a retired Utah highway Patrol. Trooper and his wife, that they had seen, heard and spoken to Butch in Kanab in the summer of 1941, thirty-two years after the episode at San Vicente. In a telephone conversation with retired UHP Trooper Merrill Johnson in August 1991, he confirmed the story and provided additional details pulled from memories of a chance encounter a half-century earlier.

Johnson said he pulled a man over for speeding about seventeen miles north of Kanab in mid-July 1941. He then continued his shift and headed home. As he pulled into the driveway, he was surprised to see the same car he had pulled over earlier parked near his house. He and his wife were living with his father-in-law at the time. Johnson said, "When I walked into the house, I saw my father-in-law, John, in the kitchen, talking to the man I'd written the ticket to earlier in the day. The fellow was startled to see me. I was wearing my uniform, you know, and he made a move to get up from the chair, when John said, "It's all right; It's my son-in-law, he lives here, he's OK."

After the initial confusion passed, John made an announcement: "Merrill, this here's an old friend of the family, Bob Parker (Butch Cassidy) he was passing through and dropped in to say hello. Butch, this is my son-in-law, Merrill Johnsonn, and that's my daughter, Ramona, in the kitchen."

Having been introduced by his father-in-law, Johnson sat down with the two old-timers and listened as they traded reminiscences about the days of their youth in Utah.

After all of the rumors and speculation, you're left with the burden of deciding which stories you believe and which one's you don't. Among all the stories, legends and speculations there is one thing we do know for sure; Butch Cassidy and his gang put together the longest sequence of successful bank and train robberies in the history of the American West, and they gave the American people something to talk about for over 100 years.

Important Dates in Wild Bunch History

December 1861
Orlando Camillo Hanks born in De Witt County, Texas.

1864
Matt Warner (Willard Christiansen) born at Ephraim, Utah.

April 13, 1866
Butch Cassidy born in Beaver, Utah.

1867
Harvey Logan born in Tama County, Iowa.

Spring 1867
The Sundance Kid born at Upper Providence Township, Pennsylvania.

September 12, 1868
Will Carver born in Wilson County, Texas.

November 25, 1868
Elzy Lay born at Mount Pleasant, Ohio.

1870
Walter Punteney born in Frankfort, Kansas.

March 20, 1871
George Currie born in Charlottetown, Prince Edward Island, Canada.

January 5, 1874
Ben Kilpatrick born in Coleman, Texas.

August 5, 1874
Sundance Kid pleads guilty of horse theft in Sundance, Wyoming and is sentenced to eighteen months.

February 4, 1889
Sundance Kid pardoned by Wyoming Governor Thomas Moonlight.

June 24, 1889
Butch Cassidy, Matt Warner, and Tom McCarty rob San Miguel Valley Bank at Telluride, Colorado.

November 29, 1892
The Sundance Kid, Bill Madden, and Harry Bass rob Great Northern Train near Malta, Montana.

July 4, 1894
Butch Cassidy receives two years sentence for horse theft.

December 27, 1894
Harvey Logan (Kid Curry) kills Pike Landusky at Landusky, Montana.

January 6, 1896
Butch Cassidy released from Wyoming State Penitentiary.

May 7, 1896
Matt Warner, William Wall, and E. B. Coleman Kill David Milton and Ike Staunton.

August 13, 1896
Butch Cassidy, Elzy Lay, and Bub Meeks rob bank at Montpelier, Idaho.

September 21, 1896
Matt Warner and William Wall convicted of manslaughter and sentenced to five years in the Utah Penitentiary for killing David Milton and Ike Staunton. Coleman acquitted.

April 21, 1897
Butch Cassidy, Elzy Lay, Bub Meeks, and Joe Walker rob payroll office of Pleasant Valley Coal Company at Castle Gate, Utah.

June 28, 1897
Sundance Kid, George Currie, Harvey Logan, Walt Punteney, and Tom O'Day rob bank at Belle Fourche, South Dakota. O'Day captured.

September 22, 1897
Sundance Kid, Harvey Logan, and Walt Punteney captured by sheriff John Dunn near Lavina, Montana.

October 31, 1897
Sundance Kid, Harvey Logan, Walt Punteney, and Tom O'Day escape from Deadwood, South Dakota jail.

November 2, 1897
Walt Punteney and Tom O'Day recaptured near Spearfish, South Dakota.

April 3, 1899
Sundance Kid, George Currie, and Harvey Logan rob the Club Saloon in Elko, Nevada.

June 2, 1899
George Currie, Harvey Logan, and Sundance Kid rob Union Pacific train near Nevada.

June 5, 1899
Carbon County Sheriff Joe Hazen shot and killed by Wilcox train robbers.

July 11, 1899
Sam Ketchum, Elzy Lay, and Will Carver rob Colorado Southern train near Folsom, New Mexico.

July 16, 1899
Huerfano County, New Mexico, Sheriff Edward Farr shot and killed by Folsom robbers. Sam Ketchu wounded and captured.

July 24, 1899
Sam Ketchum dies of blood poisoning at Santa Fe.

August 22, 1899
Elzy Lay arrested by Eddy Country, New Mexico, Sheriff M. C. Stewart.

October 10, 1899
Elzy Lay sentenced to life in prison.

January 21, 1900
Matt Warner released from Utah Penitentiary.

February 28, 1900
Lonnie Logan shot and killed by Pinkerton detectives at Dodson, Missouri.

April 17, 1900
George Currie shot and killed near Greenriver, Utah, by Sheriff Jesse Tyler and Sheriff William Preece.

August 29, 1900
Union Pacific train robbed near Tipton, Wyoming. Butch Cassidy, Sundance Kid, and Harvey Logan and others have been named as suspects.

September 19, 1900
Winnemucca, Nevada, bank robbed. Butch Cassidy, Sundance Kid, and Will Carver suspected of robbery.

November 21, 1900
Sundance Kid, Will Carver, Ben Kilpatrick, Harvey Logan, and Butch Cassidy have group photograph taken at Fort Worth, Texas.

Early January 1901
Sundance Kid and Etta (Ethel) Place visit Longabaugh family in Pennsylvania.

February 1, 1901
Sundance Kid, Etta Place, and Butch Cassidy check into Mrs. Catherine Taylor's boarding house in New York City.

February 20, 1901
Butch Cassidy, Sundance Kid, and Etta Place leave New York aboard the British Ship Herminius.

Late March 1901
Butch Cassidy, Sundance Kid, and Etta Place arrive in Buenos Aries, Argentina.

April 2, 1901
Will Carver killed at Sonora, Texas, by Sheriff E. S. Briant.

July 3, 1901
Harvey Logan, Ben Kilpatrick, and Camillo Hanks rob Great Northern train near Wagner, Montana.

July 25, 1901
Rancher Jim Winters shot and killed from ambush at his ranch near Landusky, Montana. Harvey Logan suspected by killing Winters as revenge for Winters 1896 Killing of Johnny Logan.

October 14, 1901
Annie Rogers, Harvey Logan's girlfriend, is arrested in Nashville, Tennessee, for passing bank notes stolen in the July 3, Great Northern robbery.

November 5, 1901
Ben Kilpatrick and girlfriend Laura Bullion arrested in St. Louis, Missouri, for passing stolen bank notes.

December 12, 1901
Ben Kilpatrick and Laura Bullion plead guilty to passing and forging stolen bank notes.

December 13, 1901
Harvey Logan shoots and seriously wounds two policemen in a Knoxville, Tennessee saloon.

December 15, 1901
Harvey Logan arrested near Jefferson City, Tennessee, and returned to Knoxville.

March 3, 1902
Sundance Kid and Etta Place sail for New York aboard the S. S. Soldier Prince.

April 2, 1902
Butch Cassidy files an application for a fourth of a square leagues of Government land within the Province of Chubut near Cholila.

April 3, 1902
Sundance Kid and Etta Place arrive in New York City.

April 16, 1902
Camillo Hanks shot and killed by police officers in a San Antonio, Texas, saloon.

June 18, 1902
Annie Rogers acquitted by a Nashville, Tennessee jury of forging and attempting to pass stolen bank notes.

July 10, 1902
Sundance Kid and Etta Place arrive in Buenos Aries.

49

November 20, 1902

Harvey Logan convicted in a Knoxville, Tennessee court of forging and passing stolen bank notes.

June 27, 1903

Harvey Logan escapes the Knox County, Tennessee jail.

June 7, 1904

Harvey Logan and two accomplices rob Denver & Rio Grande train No. 5 near Parachute, Colorado.

June 9, 1904

Harvey Logan commits suicide after being wounded in a shootout with posse.

1904/1905: Etta Place returns to the United States.

May 1905

Butch Cassidy and Sundance Kid make arrangements to sell their livestock and buildings, they did not yet hold clear title to the land, before leaving Cholila.

July, 4 1905

Elzy Lay's sentence commuted to ten years by New Mexico Governor Miguel A. Otero.

September 19, 1905

Laura Bullion released from the Missouri State Penitentiary at Jefferson City, Missouri.

December 19, 1905

Butch Cassidy and Sundance Kid rob bank at Villa Mercedes, Argentina.

January 10, 1906
Elzy Lay released from prison.

Mid 1907
Butch Cassidy and the Sundance Kid working at the Concordia Tin Mines, Bolivia.

November 4, 1908
Butch Cassidy and Sundance Kid steal Aramayo mine payroll near Tupiza.

November 6, 1908
Butch Cassidy and Sundance Kid killed by Bolivian soldiers at San Vicente, Bolivia (maybe).

May 29, 1911
Ben Kilpatrick released from the federal penitentiary at Atlanta, Georgia.

March 12, 1912
Ben Kilpatrick killed during the robbery of a GH &SA train near Sanderson, Texas.

November 10, 1934
Elzy Lay passes away in Los Angeles, California, age 65.

December 21, 1938
Matt Warner passes away in Utah at age 74.

1949
Walt Punteney passes away in Pinedale, Wyoming.

Additional Apricot Press Books

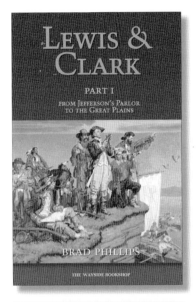

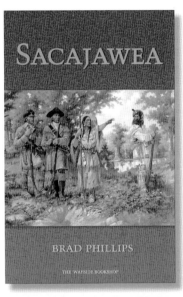

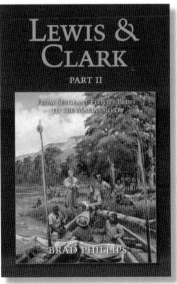

Order Online! www.apricotpress.com

Apricot Press Order Form

Book Title	Quantity	x	Cost / Book	=	Total

All Cook Books are $9.95 US.   **All Other Books are $6.95 US.**

Do not send Cash. Mail check or money order to:
**Apricot Press   P.O. Box 1611
American Fork, Utah   84003**
Telephone 801-756-0456
Allow 3 weeks for delivery.

**Quantity discounts available.
Call us for more information.**
9 a.m. - 5 p.m. MST

Sub Total =

Shipping = $2.00

Tax 8.5% =

Total Amount
Enclosed =

Shipping Address

Name:

Street:

City: State:

Zip Code:

Telephone:

Email: